# *Batu-Angas*

# *Batu-Angas*

*Envisioning nature with*
*Alfred Russel Wallace*

Anne Cluysenaar

**seren**

Seren is the book imprint of
Poetry Wales Press Ltd
57 Nolton Street, Bridgend, CF31 3AE, Wales
www.seren-books.com

ISBN 978-1-85411-464-8



A CIP record for this title is available from the British Library.



*The publisher works with the financial assistance of the Welsh Books Council.*

Cover image: 'Wallace's Standard wing' by Robert Gilmor, donated by the artist

Printed in Plantin by Bell & Bain Ltd, Glasgow

"...if we continue to devote our chief energies to the utilising of our knowledge of the laws of nature with the view of still further extending our commerce and our wealth, the evils which necessarily accompany these when too eagerly pursued, may increase to such gigantic dimensions as to be beyond our power to alleviate."

– Alfred Russel Wallace, *The Malay Archipelago*, 1869

Wallace in 1848, shortly before he left for the Amazon

# FOREWORD

"THAT IS THE BIRTH-PLACE of Alfred Russel Wallace". Little did I imagine at the time that this sentence would result for me in several years' poetic participation in Wallace's travels through Amazonia and the Malay Archipelago. Few of us on that field trip knew much about Wallace. Our leader, the naturalist Colin Titcombe, went on to explain that the infant brought up in the small cottage on the banks of the river Usk came to discover (at considerable risk to his own life) how flora and fauna evolve through processes of natural selection. At the time, my only association with the name of Wallace was through a bird of paradise. Later, when I was already engaged on the present sequence, Colin passed me a printed copy of the painting which now graces the cover of this book.

As I read *My Life*, Wallace's autobiography, I found myself enthralled by the character of the man, a delightful blend of determination, modesty, open-mindedness and a quite unshakeable love for life. At the same time I felt a difference between his driving passion and my own. From early youth onwards, Wallace recognised in himself above all "a strong desire to know the causes of things". Questioning my own awareness, I recognised my predominant passion to be for life itself, as it exists before me. So I became aware that the questions driving Wallace's life have been largely absent from my own, while my immediate response to living things would, from childhood on, have made it impossible for me to kill specimens for study. All the same, it was now clear to me that only through studying his collections could Wallace come to realise that natural selection works through differences within species – a realisation which may yet enable us not only to preserve threatened species but also to make sense of human origins and potential. So the very life I respond to so intensely as a poet needs humanity to embrace, for nature's protection, and for our own, insights provided through scientific research. Can poetry and the other arts, then, be seen to have any role to play in evolution, past and to come?

In the opening three poems of the sequence, I posed myself

questions with regard to 'the tenuous job of poet'. The arts have certainly played, in human existence, a prominent role. But why? Seen in the context of evolution, it seems clear that, to play such a role, artistic responses and occupations must bear on group (and also personal) survival. It struck me that, in the present century, it may be more important than ever to understand how the functionings of matter have enabled humanity to emerge not only physically but also intellectually and spiritually. Deep time stretches on either side of our present existence. Perhaps modern scientific insights need to be accompanied by arts capable of facing these dizzying perspectives in terms that enable us to keep our emotional balance.

Wallace knew the importance of the arts and argued for their right to engage with science. An early lecture on 'The Advantages of Varied Knowledge' contains the following passage:

> What pleasure would remain for the enthusiastic artist were he forbidden to gaze upon the face of nature, and transfer her loveliest scenes to his canvas? or for the poet were the means denied him to recue from oblivion the passing visions of his imagination? or to the chemist were he snatched from his laboratory ere some novel experiment were concluded, or some ardently pursued theory confirmed? or to any of us were we compelled to forego some intellectual pursuit that was bound up with our every thought? And here we see the advantage possessed by him whose studies have been in various directions.

He goes on to argue for the contribution scientific perspectives may make to the immediate enjoyment of life:

> He who has extended his enquiries into the varied phenomena of nature learns to despise no fact however small... He sees in every dewdrop trembling on the grass causes at work analogous to those which have produced the spherical figure of the earth and planets; and in the beautiful forms of crystallization on his window-panes on a frosty morning he recognises the action of laws which may also have a part in the production of the similer forms of plants and of many of the lower animal types. Thus the simplest facts of everyday life have to him an inner meaning....

As I followed Wallace in his travels, I began to find that my perception of plants and creatures, and of our own lives among them, was indeed acquiring new perspectives. Reading his books, seeing and handling his specimens, talking with biologists engaged in their own current research (sometimes derived in part from Wallace's own), enriched my sense of what could be seen on our small farm in the Welsh borders and deepened my enjoyment of life. I hope that some of this enrichment and joy is at least hinted at in *Batu-Angas*.

But why that title? It was during an acute bout of malaria on the volcanic island of Ternate that it 'flashed upon' Wallace how life evolves through natural selection. When he could hold a pen, Wallace explained his ideas to Charles Darwin – the two men had for some time been in correspondence – and asked whether he saw merit in them. The letter was a shock to the older naturalist. He had been accumulating evidence for many years but had so far published nothing on the subject. In due course, independent but similar insights penned by Wallace and Darwin were put before the Linnean Society in London on July 1, 1858. And the title of this book? From the local language of Ternate itself, Wallace had borrowed the phrase 'batu-angas' to describe the 'burnt rocks' or cooled lava he saw there. The phrase struck me as a suitable title for the sequence because it could be said to symbolise the visible world at any one time – a world now, thanks to Wallace and Darwin, known to maintain a seeming stasis only, amid the flowing lava of evolution. I hope the phrase may also draw attention to Wallace's grasp of crucial interactions between biology and geography, a grasp which has led to his being recognised today as 'the father of biogeography'. It was thanks to this insight that he proposed what is now called 'the Wallace line' running between islands associated with either Asia or Australia, the land on either side being marked by distinctive flora and fauna – and it turns out that much of what he noticed, there and elsewhere, derives from the tearing apart or collision of continental plates as they slide over the molten core of this planet.

Poems in the sequence are linked to each other through the exploration and transformation of intertwined themes rather than by narrative or strictly biographical sequence. My hope for them is that they will prove capable of creating spaces open to the reader's own observations on nature, and on the nature of human life.

Anne Cluysenaar

Wallace in Singapore, 1862

# INTRODUCTION

ONCE UPON A TIME, some one hundred years ago, the British polymath Alfred Russel Wallace (1823-1913) was just about the most famous scientist in the world. He had earned this place – he was often referred to late in life as the 'Grand Old Man of Science' – through a career that had stretched into eight decades and touched on matters as diverse as evolutionary biology and spiritualism, glacial theory and land planning, and biogeography and monetary policy. To all these subjects and several more he made notable contributions, but he is now most remembered for his independent discovery of the principle of natural selection in 1858 and the way that discovery prompted Charles Darwin to get going and write *The Origin of Species*. Darwin ended up receiving most of the credit for the idea, however, and despite Wallace's many period crusades he was quickly forgotten to all but a few specialists when he died in November 1913, just before the start of World War I.

There was nearly total silence on the subject of Wallace for forty-five years, but the 1958 centennial celebration of the first presentation of the natural selection concept reawakened interest in him. Slowly but surely the attention level has been increasing, including the recent publication of a slew of excellent biographies. But the story as it has been presented to date is far from complete. Fundamental questions still exist both as to the ultimate value of his ideas, and how he came to them.

The basic chronology of events of Wallace's life is reasonably well known. He was born at Llanbadoc, near Usk near the boundary of Wales and England to poor middle-class English parents in 1823, but at the age of five he and his family moved to Hertford, where he was eventually forced to leave school at age thirteen to take up a trade. For a number of years he toiled for an older brother as a surveyor and builder in the West of England and the South of Wales, but then was let go during a work slowdown. In early 1844 he picked up a position as a master at a school in Leicester, where by chance he met another young man, Henry Walter Bates, who was interested in beetle collecting. Wallace had already undertaken some amateurish natural history studies, both in England and in Wales, but now his enthusiasm for field work grew. When his older brother died suddenly in early 1845 he returned to Wales to take over his surveying business there, but it was only a matter of time before he suggested to Bates that they turn professional as collectors. In early 1848 the two set off for the Amazon.

By this time Wallace had already become a convert to the idea of organic evolution. It was quickly apparent to him, however, that no one seemed to have a workable idea as to what mechanism might be underlying the process. Wallace and Bates made it their business in the Amazon to find out, but after four years an answer had eluded them. Bates remained in South America until 1859, but in 1852 Wallace, weak from various illnesses, left and returned to English soil to ponder his next move.

Within eighteen months he was on the go again, this time to the Indonesia region, then referred to as the 'Malay Archipelago'. There he met with great success, not only as a collector and observer of natural history and native peoples, but also as a theorist. In 1855 he published a paper that neatly summarized the patterns of correlation in time and space between extinct and living forms; this all but founded outright the modern approach to the field of biogeography, which examines "what animals and plants live where, and why". Shortly thereafter his efforts brought to attention a sharp discontinuity between the biotas of western and central Indonesia and those lands to the east, a boundary which is now known as 'Wallace's Line'. And, in 1858, there came the crowning discovery: natural selection – the 'survival of the fittest', thought out while he was resting during a malarial fit. When Wallace wrote up a short essay describing his idea and sent it off to Charles Darwin and another naturalist, geologist Charles Lyell, "for comment", he guaranteed his admission to the highest ranks of scientific company on his return. This took place four years later in 1862; by then the 1859 publication of Darwin's *The Origin of Species* had stirred up a firestorm of discussion, and Wallace soon found himself at the very center of it.

But in being styled a 'Darwinist' it seems that Wallace had been somewhat incompletely understood. While in fact agreeing with Darwin on most matters, he was not ready to go so far as extending his support to the full reaches of Darwinian thinking. There is no indication, especially, that Wallace ever believed the higher attributes of human nature had emerged through natural selection. Eventually this schism led him to adopt Spiritualism in 1866, and from that point onward he would also differ from Darwin on a number of other matters in evolutionary theory ranging from the effectiveness of sexual selection (that is, as to whether female choice at the animal level was a significant selecting force) to certain biogeographic questions.

For some fifteen years Wallace gave most of his time to a range of scientific questions, but in the late 1870s he began to expand his focus to matters of social concern. He became a leading advocate of land reform, co-founding the Land Nationalisation Society in 1880 and becoming its first President (he remained in the office through to his death in 1913). He also wrote extensively on subjects as varied as the disposition of wills and trusts, women's suffrage, trade barriers, monetary standards, war spending, the treatment of labor, vaccination practices, socialism, reform of the House of Lords, philosophical questions of 'might vs. right', rural depopulation, poverty, adulteration of manufactured goods, foreign loans, and social duty. These interventions did not exactly endear him to most of the power brokers of the period, but the rank and file increasingly came to feel – rightly – that he was on their side.

It is this combined career trajectory that makes Wallace one of the most fascinating and inspiring figures in intellectual history. In a 1901 review of his *Studies Scientific and Social* the great American philosopher Charles Peirce referred to him thusly:

> Not quite a typical man of science is Wallace; not a man who observes and studies only because he is eager to learn, because he is conscious that his actual conceptions and theories are inadequate, and he feels a need of being set right; nor yet one of those men who are so dominated by a sense of the tremendous importance of a truth in their possession that they are borne on to propagate it by all means that God and nature have put into their hands no matter what, so long as it be effective. He is rather a man conscious of superior powers of sound and solid reasoning, which enable him to find paths to great truths that other men could not, and also to put the truth before his fellows with a demonstrative evidence that another man could not bring out; and along with this there is a moral sense, child-like in its candor, manly in its vigor, which will not allow him to

> approve anything illogical or wrong, though it be upon his own side of a question which stirs the depths of his moral nature.

A good indication of the depth of Wallace's concern for his fellow man can be drawn from the stirring final words of an essay he composed in 1906 – at the age of eighty-three – regarding "the Native Problem":

> For nearly twelve years I travelled and lived mostly among uncivilised or completely savage races, and I became convinced that they all possessed good qualities, some of them in a very remarkable degree, and that in all the great characteristics of humanity they are wonderfully like ourselves. Some, indeed, among the brown Polynesians especially, are declared by numerous independent and unprejudiced observers, to be both physically, morally, and intellectually our equals, if not our superiors; and it has always seemed to me one of the disgraces of our civilisation that these fine people have not in a single case been protected from contamination by the vices and follies of our more degraded classes, and allowed to develope their own social and political organism under the advice of some of our best and wisest men and the protection of our world wide power. That would have been indeed a worthy trophy of our civilisation. What we have actually done, and left undone, resulting in the degradation and lingering extermination of so fine a people, is one of the most pathetic of its tragedies.

I have been a close student of Wallace's work and life for some thirty years, and never cease to be amazed at the breadth and solidity of his vision, whether it lead the student in scientific or social/moral directions. I believe I can fully understand Ms. Cluysenaar's desire to express the effect of his inspiration in poetical form; certainly the events of his life provide the poet with ample opportunities for engagement. Wallace himself enjoyed (and actually wrote some) poetry, moreover, and I'm sure he would be quite pleased to be remembered in this fashion.

Charles H. Smith

# THE POEMS

*Ornithoptera croesus croesus*,
a Wallace specimen of this birdwing butterly

# I

"During my very first walk into the forest at Batchian, I had seen sitting on a leaf out of reach, an immense butterfly..."
– Alfred Russel Wallace, *The Malay Archipelago*

*At The Natural History Museum, London*
*– for George Beccaloni, entomologist*

Pinned on the tray,
his wings outspread,
still and dry:
*Ornithoptera croesus croesus.*

'This may be the actual one'
you tell me, angling the glass –
the sooty texture
of immense wings
dazzles by its darkness.

Somewhere on the body
forensic signs, maybe,
of Wallace's careful fingers
as he drew this butterfly, living,
from the net? And his own heart
sent blood rushing,
so that "I felt
much more like fainting
than I have done
when in apprehension
of immediate death" –
all day afterwards,
ah, how his head ached!

To that Mussaenda shrub
with its white bracts and long
yellow orange-eyed blooms,
lured by scent and sight,
*croesus* will come for nectar.

Closed up, he makes just a patch
of leaf-thrown shadow,
or an oblong black-veined leaf,
yellow-green in sunlight.
Open, the bright petals
on his outspread wings –
orange sprays, yellow dots,
amid yellow and white and orange –
hold his body safe
in a bill-distracting corolla.

As I catch a trace
of Wallace's fine-tipped quill
on the tiny round of the label
and the dull glint of the pin
through that wizened thorax,
I think of a mind's movement
stilled between pages,
as dead, as rich –

ready in another mind
to fly, and settle.

# II

"Can we believe that we are fulfilling the purpose of our existence while so many of the wonders and beauties of the creation remain unnoticed around us?"

– Alfred Russel Wallace, *My Life*

*For Torben Larsen, entomologist*

In case after case,
amazements of complex colour:
dots and stripes and swirls –
the Peruvian dazzle,
frail mica-translucence,
mercury-liquid blueness,
glass-wing come-and-go glitter.

It's the entomologists' fair,
and we've queued in October rain
for the Kempton Racecourse turnstiles,
jumping to islands between puddles,
cracking jokes with strangers.

At the trestle tables inside
it's quite hard to get a look-in,
what with these serious chaps,
boxes tucked under arms,
and the quiet observant children
unsurprised as experts.

About killing, I learned yesterday:
most often a light pinch
under raised-up wings,
the long heart constricted
to its last beat.

Among all the rest, birdwings.

Why, if Wallace's wonder –
golden-winged *croesus croesus* –
turns up, should I not buy one?
I feel hesitation beginning.

A naturalist once said to me:
'The individual doesn't matter' –
and I doubt it'll be the collector's
delight in rare acquisitions
that will one day extinguish species,
or the scientist's need to test
theory by close observation –
which may, rather, help to save them.

It's logging, it's slash and burn.
Smoke stifling the forest.
Commerce. And desperation.

And I too have needed a body –
something more dead than a photo –
to bring me the sense of his life
ancient, single, and other.

Those glaucus solid mounds
that gave him mosaic vision,
colours that still reflect
his favourite yellow flowers,
hind-wing edges, silky
with hair-like scales, that combed
the lek with a sexual perfume.

I think of your hands showing,
like this, how he'd rise from beneath,
touching his body to hers,
and her antennae tilt to smell
his personal scent, the hairs
and pheromone hind-wing patches,
intimate under her feet.

'The taste of this one?' Choosing.

What need do I still have,
        now, to possess a body,
                having sensed (overhear myself think this)
                        a soul – what better word is there?

On the train home, I turn
    the pages of second-hand books
            purchased instead – facts and photos;
wonder, dozing a little,
        at the tenuous job of poet.

# III

"There is one other fact connected with my mental nature which may be worth noticing here...an often-repeated dream..."

– Alfred Russel Wallace, *My Life*

I've startled myself into silence.
Well, not silence quite, but
versions of a possible poem
that refuse to become one.
The subject stays outside,
pointed at, independent,
not that undiscovered place
words should lead into.

But Wallace's dream is there somewhere:
the way that little boy lay
in bed asleep,
listening with inner ears
to a distant beating or flapping,
"some creature with huge wings",
the sound coming nearer and nearer.

He'd wait for the deep thud
and the sudden silence,
seeming to feel the creature
"clinging with its wings outspread
against the wall of the house
just outside my window",
seeking a way in.

"I was afraid", he says,
but then he would wake ("usually"!)
and listen to a different silence,
one he could fall asleep in.

He knew it had to do with death.
Someone had shown the toddler
on a dead man's house, "a hatchment
or funeral escutcheon".
His young mind made of it,
he says, "an unmeaning jumble
of strange dragon-like forms
surrounded with black".

In the night within a night
of his childhood dream
he would use that magical word,
'hatchment': "The hatchment is coming;
I hope it will not get in",
the word being part of the nightmare,
and his shield against it.

Dreams – are they nature's poems,
virtual hints for survival?

Encouraged by the thought,
(and now by where this is leading)
I see how right that dream was
for Wallace, nature's explorer.

That unmeaning jumble of forms
clinging at his window-sill.

The winged image, prophetic.

Mobbed by Curl-crested Toucans

# IV

"...I possessed a strong desire to know the causes of things, a great love of beauty in form and colour, and a considerable but not excessive desire for order..."

– Alfred Russel Wallace, *My Life*

Like a scatter of tiles in mid air:
Tut-tut! Tut-tut! Tut-tut-tut!
High up in our thorn-tree's branches
his black shape quite distorted
by gestures of possession.
I am invading his space
and he knows enough to be angry.

I look up to meet his stare
the second when spluttering breaks
to a phrase of song.

Shocked, we both stop still
in a sunlight that truly now
feels like the sunlight of spring.

What stays with me is this –
the feel of where we both were:
my foot about to step on,
his wings bunching to fly,
but still this tension between us –
caught up by an impulse we couldn't
have guessed at before it happened.

I find myself thinking of Wallace,
a hunter shouldering his gun
as the only means of touching.

How often his fingers unfolded
loose wings, tilted to the light
brilliances now without function,
while his palm felt the warm weight
of a silenced breast,
the dry roughness of claws
crumpled on a branch of air.

I share the smell of blood
while I reach for his understandings.

# V

"I wanted to go again to the top of the Beacons to see if I would find any rare beetles there, and also to show my brother the waterfalls...Starting after an early breakfast we walked to Pont-nedd-fychan, and then turned up the western branch to the Rocking Stone... It was here I obtained one of the most beautiful British beetles, *Trichius fasciatus*, the only time I ever captured it."

– Alfred Russel Wallace, *My Life*

*For Matthew Lethbridge, who showed me Saturn*

On the phone to Entomology
from the desk in the vast hall
(Diplodocus behind me)
I mention these poems on Wallace.
In no time, I'm up the stairs.
At the door, a friendly welcome.
The big packed spaces.

I explain my mission – to see
the beetle *Trichius fasciatus*.
Foot and Mouth has put out of bounds
the Rocking Stone, where Wallace
found it in early youth.

They slide out a case, and there
is a row of the woolly beetles.
"I've never seen it alive.
If you ever find one, would you
consider sending it here?"

I imagine how I might spot
in a dandelion or a hawkweed,
shiny wing-cases patterned
as if with petals – a brightness
hidden away in brightness.

I remember the Kogi Indians,
how a boy is transformed to a shaman,
He's shut away in a cave,

for many years, in darkness...
They tell him about the world
but he never sees it. One day,
before dawn, they bring him
out.

He sees the world becoming
while he becomes, his body
stretching, filling with light,
threaded with wings, with veils
of drifting white, the flow
of sky down there in the
depth.

Knowing is never enough.
We have to see – like seeing,
through a telescope, the rings
of Saturn, ordinary Earth
transformed under our feet.

A bee chafer beetle (*Trichius fasciatus*)

# VI

"The first epiphytal orchid I ever saw was at a flower show in Swansea, where Mr. D.J. Dillwyn Llewellyn exhibited a plant of *Epidendrum fragrans*, one of the less attractive kinds, but which yet caused in me a thrill of enjoyment which no other plant in the show produced.... This and other references to and descriptions of (orchids) gave them, in my mind, a weird and mysterious charm ...and ...had its share in producing that longing for the tropics which a few years later was satisfied in the equatorial forests of the Amazon."

– Alfred Russel Wallace, *My Life*

*Visiting Alan Gregg at The Swansea Botanical Complex,*
*Singleton Park*

On a bitter October day,
after months of waiting, you ring
to say: 'The plant is in flower'
but warn: 'You'll be disappointed'.

Half way down the long middle shelf
of the orchid house, you point
to a spray of leaves. The roots,
are silvered, shiny-green tipped,
and reach not for earth but air.
The flower is whiteish, small,
and 'weird' indeed, with its lip
held above not below the petals.

But the dizzying vanilla sweetness!

Back home, a December moon,
full, white as a furnace,
burns with reflected light.
Now the spray you cut, on the sill,
set in an egg-cup of water,
withholds every trace of scent.

And that most signals its life.

An Amzonian tree, drawn by Wallace

Despite the severance, despite
this domestic air, it still
recalls its own hemisphere –
the need for sunlight to warm
chilled wings in the canopy,
and activate millenia.

Next day, when our winter sun
strikes through the double-glazing
and I shut my eyes, this room
is the forest its genes imagine.

# VII

"Our greatest treasure was the beautiful clear-winged butterfly – the *Haetera esmeralda*...caught for the first time."
– Alfred Russel Wallace, *Travels on the Amazon*

He notes: "Very few insects".

Then something catches his eye.

It reflects, but only just,
a far off light of sky
above the cut-leaf canopy.
As if, under vertical sun,
in gloom over fallen leaves
air were to twist and pinch
around brilliant petals, drifting.

This is the living form
of the rainforest's age, an art
grown of its interactions,
which now he has gathered up
into a triangle, dying,
that knowledge folded away.

Our knowledge a little greater.

In a butterfly farm near Kew
clear-wings, hatched under glass,
make eggs filled with memories.

Immobile, their wings are windows
to leaves, paths and placards.
In flight, two separate petals
float, purple-pink, disrupting
the see-through wandering wing-beat.

# VIII

"But what lovely yellow flower is that suspended in the air between two trunks, yet far from either? It shines in the gloom as if its petals were gold."

– Alfred Russel Wallace, *Travels on the Amazon*

*At the Herbarium, Kew*

"I can show you a model
of the likeliest one." He brings me
a cluster of dusty wax
from which a yellowish blob
bounces on a black wire.

Among the books, in a light
meant for reading, no such wonder
is even imaginable.

But then, he who has seen it
in virgin forest,
tells me about the bees,
bees that are territorial.

In May, in the flooded Gapo,
one travels as if suspended
above the Earth. Still water
falls away, amber, below you.
You're forty feet up. The canopy
brushes the prow of your boat.

And now, for a moment, you see
what the bees see – an intruder
flying across their space.

They attack and the sticky pollinia
find wings to the next *Oncidium*!

Now I see where the model fails.

Made for display on a table
it has to forgo the thing –
the very thing – which the plant
lives by: that "slender wire
a yard and a half long".
Which Wallace measured. Which allowed
the flower to fly. Which, remembered,
made him see in the present tense.

# IX

"I soon found that the Cocks of the Rock, to obtain which was my chief object in coming here, were not to be found near the village. Their principal resort was the Serra de Cobati...situated some ten or twelve miles off in the forest...I could not have imagined such serrated rocks to exist."

– Alfred Russel Wallace, *Travels on the Amazon*

When the body was put in his hands,
he stared, "lost in admiration".

"Not a spot of blood was visible,
not a feather was ruffled,... the soft
warm, flexible body set off
the fresh, swelling plumage
in a manner which no stuffed
specimen can approach".

He risks his life for this –
the collecting of specimens.

This time, the Serra's crags,
climbed by roots and creepers.
Gorges. Granite ridges.
And now, here it was – the first
of a series. Had he begun,
already, to guess the role
of differences within species?

As I write this, thud – a bird
hits my open window-pane.
Now its head rolls on my palm.
Young sparrow, fully fledged,
its beak yellow at the join.
Had it seemed to see a sky
beyond, some open space?

A Cock of the Rock

I was about to remember
    my visit to Tring –
how, as I sat at the bench
    (sun through the slatted blinds)
        there came that blaze of orange.

A tray of Cocks of the Rock.
    Cylinders stuffed. The legs
        neatly laid back. The heads
            stretched out straight, on their chins,
                a pose unknown in life.

This one here may well be his first.
    It lies stiff in my palm. Its eyes
        are bulbs of pale smooth cotton.
This could be the one he glimpsed,
    perched in its "gloomy thicket" –
        "a magnificent bird...shining out
            like a mass of brilliant flame".

And what did the bird see?
    A tall man raising a stick?

## X

"...we passed by a high cliff, on which were some of the picture writings I had so much wished to see...I took a general sketch of the whole, and some accurate tracings of the more curious figures, which have unfortunately been since lost."

– Alfred Russel Wallace, *Travels on the Amazon*

The pencil tip carries
        the weight of his fingers.

He copies lines from the wave,
        the grey wave of stone,
                that hangs above him.

This is the Rock of Creation.

Arms and legs akimbo,
        out of the hidden depth,
                the roots of earth,
                        they come, dancing
or is it sinking?
        Spreadeagled, crying out,
                hands and eyes wide –
either way, their backs
        are always to the mystery,
but their transparent bodies,
        between the lines, are full of it.

He copies the bulge of belly,
        the round of head,
                essentials without any shading.
Eleven thousand years
        between him and whoever
                got up there somehow,
                        as if flying, and drew
                                humans coming or going,
and a rayed red circle, fat
        with yellow light.

Through that, nothing shows. It is.
        And it still dazzles.

A chain of moments.
        Hands, one after another,
                reaching to an empty surface.

Caught in their time.
        Making their mark.

Wallace's copies of cliff drawings

# XI

"In the evening I took my gun, and strolled along the road a little way into the forest, at the place I had so long looked forward to reaching, and was rewarded by falling in with one of the lords of the soil, which I had long wished to encounter."
– Alfred Russel Wallace, *Travels on the Amazon*

He should have known better
than to walk off, as night fell,
alone, armed only with small-shot.

He had seen life draw its distinctions
on one shore this,
on the other that –
and here was the place
where those two great rivers rise,
Amazon, Orinoko.
Their watershed.
And he goes here barefoot
after small prey. Hungry, yes,
but this is the kind of mistake
that reflects a wish.

Where else but here
should he meet that slow
black shape filling out
from the forest edge, long and low,
and stock still, now, blocking the road,
its great head turning?
Strung tight between them
a double gaze,
life beholding itself.

Knowing he must not shoot
(small-shot would only enrage)
he stands in silence, admiring –
in what may be final moments –
this rare black jaguar,
this "lord of the soil".

Having "fallen in" with it
        he knows himself better now
                than ever he could before.
                        At the watershed, he is prey.

His own word for it: "encounter".

An Amazonian Black Jaguar

A forest stream, from *Travels on the Amazon*

# XII

"I had now reached the furthest point in this direction that I had wished to attain."

– Alfred Russel Wallace, *Travels on the Amazon*

This is the turning-point
"where the streams divide".

He arrives at night
through virgin forest, crossing
invisible courses, the drop
unknown beneath him.

On the day he gets to Javitá
the winter season begins.
Early. It's February.
At home, spring is preparing.
Here, the waters rise,
There are fish in the branches.

He plans to stay forty days.

He knows that the white man,
the 'rational', catching
butterflies, beetles –
folding away onto paper
grey ghosts of the fish
he will eat for his supper –
only makes sense (if
ever) in a different world.

By the time light fades,
his hands barely hold the pencil,
red and swollen from sandflies.
He soaks them in cold water.
Iambic pentameter drifts,
phrases forming, unforming,
in place of good conversation.

Night after night
rain falls. The poem reaches
into his mind. The fear
of ignoble motives. The hope
of earning his own respect.

Must the joys of intellect
go with "the complicated villanies
of man called civilised",
"intense mental agonies",
"the long death-struggle
for the means to live",
while humans, here, go naked,
"bright and smooth", untrammelled
by "longing after gold"?

Temptations to stay for life...

That "distant dear-loved home"...

Putting down his pen,
he prepares two cups of salt.
Tomorrow's bargain-stuff.

One of Wallace's drawings of Amazonian fish

## XIII

"About two days after we left I had a slight attack of fever, and almost thought that I was still doomed to be cut off by the dread disease which had sent my brother and so many of my country-men to graves upon a foreign shore."

– Alfred Russel Wallace, *Travels on the Amazon*

Masts and shrouds flaming
in mid Atlantic. A violent swell.
Orders to take to the boats.
Suffering from yellow fever,
he slips down a rope, tearing
skin from his weakened fingers.

The ship is a cauldron of fire.

Then dawn. And an empty sea.

After-images. Monkeys
leap into the flames. A parrot
clings to a burning rope.

But emotion somehow is absent.

The boat leaks. He bales.
His hands burn with salt.

Raw pork to eat, and water
scarce. They are always thirsty.
Scorched by the sun, their heads
peel. They are drenched, sleepless.
After a week, their ration
of water must be reduced.

He lies on his back at night,
watching for meteors. By day,
he continues his observations:

Dolphins surround the boat
with "gorgeous metallic hues
of green, blue and gold".
Sometimes the sea is filled
with Medusae, oval or round,
so "beautifully contructed".
And, once, the water shines green
over a mountain peak.

They caught, he adds, several dolphins,
"not bad eating" – but Wallace,
with his eye for life in its context,
didn't see much to admire
in the colours of a dying dolphin,
evokes, instead, yet again,
the colours of the living beast
"seen in...blue transparent water".

But, when at last a ship
picks them up, and he crawls on deck,
the hope of life overcomes him.
Almost. He feels his losses:
the notebooks, specimens, drawings.
"Unknown and beautiful species"
elude even memory now.
"Now everything was gone".

To a friend he wrote that he knew
he must focus his mind on "the state
of things which actually existed".

A four spot orb weaver spider (*Araneus quadratus*)
feeding on a dragonfly

# XIV

"...so many of the laws which govern the universe and which influence our lives are, by us, unknown..."
– Alfred Russel Wallace, *My Life*

At times, it is like this:

On an island of nettles, for instance,
*Araneus quadratus*, full of eggs,
hung from her dewy wheel,
upside-down on its tensions,
the green and the white of her
a multi-millenial meditation
on how to make use of a world
invisibly far beyond,
but drifting survival her way.

Sometimes I'd catch her circling
on air-bright spokes, with dot
and dot and dot and dot
fixing her inward spiral.
More often already ensconced
where vibrations may reach her.

Long dead, this February,
she'll have left her offspring here
though the nettles are crumpled, now,
to thin grey stalks by the frost.
Later, I'll look again
for another such messenger,
oblivious of me but telling,
with each glistening resiliant
perfectly-spaced thread,
how little may need to be known,
how much more already is.

As I watch her spin, there'll come
        that image again, of our species
                exploring the means of survival:
hands disposing dead limbs,
        hands laying leaves and flowers,
                hands gifting goat-horn, amber.

# XV

"The river in front of our house was the Usk, a fine stream on which we often saw men fishing in coracles..."
– Alfred Russel Wallace, *My Life*

On the Usk, no coracles now.
Those boats that he loved for their lineage
"perhaps from the Neolithic"
are gone, with much of the fishing.

Watching the flow of the Usk,
it's as if I can see his fists –
those big hands tiny then –
gripped round an old pan-handle.
His brother John holds down
the toddler's heels as he scoops
from a massive projecting boulder
into the swirl of shallows.
A silver twist of young lampreys
carried on the current, taps
so lightly, tugs on the metal.

In his eighties Wallace recalled them,
those "snake-like" primitive fish –
how good, fried up for his tea!
Though by its "sucking mouth"
the lamprey "sticks on the hand"
(as it holds to a fish it battens on)
he thought it most "wholesome food",
plentiful then in our rivers,
and wondered that some wouldn't eat it.

Already he loved the 'beyond'.
From the neat little house he'd explore
down to the river or up
the bank, "steep and wooded", behind it.

Tall trees still pierce the canopy,
give a look of Amazon forest.

One day, the brothers set out,  
inspired by Sandford and Merton,  
with matchbox, salt and potatoes,  
build a fire, cook their potatoes,  
split the skins wide in their palms,  
sprinkle the salt and feast.

Between the house and the church  
(where the Wallace children were christened)  
there's a quarry, quite overgrown,  
its presence now largely forgotten.  
They enjoyed the "fearful delight"  
of blasting and, from a safe distance,  
the "cloud of the smaller stones".

On a rainy day, I climbed there,  
slipping, cutting my palms.  
I couldn't see much, but my fingers  
picked out from a litter of stones  
fossiliferous scumble – the debris  
(I've learned since) of salt shallows.  
This bank is the Usk inlier.  
While the land drifted north underwater,  
these were Silurian seas,  
evolution on land scarcely started.

What a place for Wallace to start from –  
the 'father of biogeography'!

As I turn this hand-held stone  
under the lens, it's so close  
that the smell of Wenlock limestone  
catches, acrid, in the throat.  
It wasn't for weeks that I saw them,  
in slanting light, these tight ridges:  
a trilobite – tiny reminder  
(half sunk in compacted sea-floor)  
of long-lived species. Extinct ones.

# XVI

"I first named the species as nearly as I could do so, and then laid them out to be pressed and dried. At such times I experienced the joy which every discovery of a new form of life gives to the lover of nature."

– Alfred Russel Wallace, *My Life*

Out on this open pasture,
high Welsh borderland,
speedwell, four-petalled blue,
then foxgloves, tall at the edge
of the wood, stilling the air,
and among the trees, cow-wheat,
tight-mouthed, ochre at lip.
By the bare path home,
tall woolly mullein, starred
with five-petalled yellow
and, in a shady spot
by our pond, the wasps
raiding magenta figwort...

One family, so many species.

But we're on our own.

I heave the *O.E.D.*
onto my lap: 'Hominid'?
*a family of mammals represented*
*by the single genus homo*
and 'Homo'? *the genus of which*
*man is the only species.*

In the mind's eye, a jumble of bones:
the robust, the gracile...some hips
adapted for walking...a skull
whose inner surface curves
to accommodate words.

And a brow whose eyes, deep-set,
        may have met our own.

We, the last, or latest.

Our trust, the cost of 'sapiens'.

A Dyak crossing a bridge

# XVII

"In this Archipelago there are two distinct faunas rigidly circumscribed, which differ as much as those of South America and Africa, and more than those of Europe and North America: yet there is nothing on the map or on the face of the islands to mark their limits. The boundary line often passes between islands closer than others in the same group. I believe the western part to be a separated portion of continental Asia. the eastern the fragmentary prolongation of a former Pacific continent. In mammalia and birds the distinction is marked by genera, families, and even orders confined to one region..."

– Alfred Russel Wallace, letter to H.W. Bates, January 5, 1858

*Remembering 'Jasmine, daughter of Eve'*

From Bali to Lombok. And now, at sunset,
volcanoes face each other across the strait,
incandescent in mist, ringed by clouds,
a deep fast sea running between.
Beneath, invisible pressures:
the Australian plate dipping
under Laurasia's edge and slowly,
far off, Himalayas rising.

It's nothing an eye can see
then or now. What he does see
on that rhyming shore is this –
familiar creatures gone, and strange ones
(as from another planet)
making use of familiar ground.

Strangest, those mounds of debris,
packed with thin-shelled eggs
that won't need turning,
and a hen-bird who never sits
but with her bare head tests
the temperature and, with giant feet,
adjusts inner to outer warmth:
day after day rakes off, rakes on
some stones, some twigs, some leaves, a little earth.

Whenever I cross the more recent
        shallower flood that divides
                where I've lived from where I was born,
a self I will never be
        shadows the woman I am.
                Languages ghost each other.

But flesh is sure of itself.

The mitochondrial pulse – Jasmine's labour pangs
        ten thousand years ago in Syrian savannah.
                Her capable touch still in my mother's hand.

# XVIII

"This extraordinary insect is rarely or never captured except when it comes to drink the sap of the sugar palms, when it is found by the natives when they go early in the morning to take away the bamboos which have been filled during the night."
– Alfred Russel Wallace, *The Malay Archipelago*

*For Richard Wallace, who rediscovered a specimen of Euchirus longimanus collected by Wallace, and George Beccaloni, who restored it and found it has the measurements of the individual illustrated in 'The Malay Archipelago'*

Elegantly curved, his arms
arc, pulling him forward,
stretch, feel for a grip
as he climbs along rucked branches.
He's fanning the air for sweetness,
inching his way as night
keeps hornbills perched, asleep
on locked feet as he passes.

It's the "small" one Wallace handed
to Robinson, to be drawn
"life-size": precisely caught,
the stroke of light on dimpled
muscle-attachments, edges
minutely-ridged or smooth,
tufts at the claws' taut hinges.

Now, in the case, it glows chestnut
as if it might still blend
into bark shining damp at dusk.

He must have tasted the sap
before fingers lifted him
to walk on Wallace's table
(O our one-way human knowledge!) –
a glorious joy, an amazement.

Long after Wallace's death,
in his grandson's attic, the case
seemed at first to hold little more
than the broken frittered remains.
of wonders he risked his life for,
and chose to keep by him always.

Now, with knowledge, persistence, care,
a young man's hands have restored
this extraordinary work of nature.
I might almost be watching the life
Wallace witnessed in morning light,
as it clambered between his hands.

*Euchirus longimanus* beetle, from *Malay Archipelago*

# XIX

"Just as I got home I overtook Ali returning from shooting with some birds hanging from his belt. He seemed much pleased, and said, "Look here, sir, what a curious bird!" holding out what at first completely puzzled me...I now saw that I had got a great prize, no less than a completely new form of the bird of paradise, differing most remarkably from every other known bird."

– Alfred Russel Wallace, *The Malay Archipelago*

Ali had seen, low through trees,
a swirl as of sun on water,
white streamers flicked up high
from winged shoulders. A flutter
signalling desire - in his sights
a metallic quiver, a breast
uttering its cry. Centuries
about to end, as with any
death. Time had reached forward
through change after slow change
till this came of it: feathers
to be flown like standards, raised,
tensioned in courtship, flailing
the deep forested darkness...

Wonders we can only witness
when, without us, they've happened.

Angling the body, I watch
how feathers like green scales
glitter all at once to blue
(both equally hard to see
among leaves, against tropical sky)
then suddenly catch my breath
at something so delicate, almost
invisible – how the eyeless head
is glossed, "beautifully glossed
with pale metallic violet".

Now I know the precise angle
Wallace himself held the bird at,
observant, eager and patient,
witnessing another of life's
inexplicably useless wonders.

Wallace's standard wing, male and female

Described by Wallace as 'Orang-utan attacked by hunters'

# XX

"One of my chief objects in coming to stay at Simunjon was to see the Orang-utan (or great man-like ape of Borneo) in his native haunts, to study his habits, and obtain good specimens of the different varieties and species of both sexes, and of the adult and young animals."

– Alfred Russel Wallace, *The Malay Archipelago*

Wallace saw what it needs most:
a "vast extent of unbroken...
lofty forest" through which,
almost upright, from tree to tree,
it walks, one long arm reaching
to bunch twigs in a bridge
while, with the other, it seeks
a branch to bear its weight,
swings across, then ambles off
as fast as a man can run,
with hardly a rustle to mark
its flight through the canopy.

He proved right to speculate
that these "strange creatures" ranged
more widely once, that "species...
more gigantic" still had roamed
the continent: their bones,
as far as southern China,
scattered among the debris
of our own ancestor's meals.

Did survivors learn to live
in trees, their canines a relic
of carnivorous hunts – grow small
on Sumatra and Borneo?
And now, modern man's here too,
logging gaps Orangs won't cross,
setting fires, oil-palm plantations.

Fifteen specimens Wallace shot,<br>
        and sent back home for study –<br>
as nothing to thousands dead<br>
        under twenty-first-century smoke.

Even so, he felt unease.<br>
        Uniquely, records the track<br>
                of bullets through those great bodies.<br>
"Six to a dozen" each.<br>
        Stresses "tenacity of life".

One full-grown male fell alive:<br>
        legs broken; hip, root of spine<br>
                shattered; bullets in neck and tongue.

Others made nests high up,<br>
        sensing death as a kind of sleep.

Related kinds, brother hominids,<br>
        long lost, but for Flores man,<br>
                alongside so recently.<br>
                        But now, extinct at last.

Those islands are, it seems,<br>
        emblems of Earth. A meteorite<br>
                veering. Still out of sight.

A Wallace specimen Orang utan

# XXI

“Vaguely thinking over the enormous and constant destruction...”
– Alfred Russel Wallace, *The Malay Archipelago*

Across a deep-sea strait
        the broken ends overlap
                of the ‘ring of fire’. Gamalama volcano
– three cones, younger and younger,
        push up as the plate shifts north,
                rise high above Ternate.
“Faint wreaths of smoke”
        come from the summit, while “hidden fires”
                burst out in streams of lava on forested slopes
                        or shake the crust over that molten core.

Hot and cold fits of fever
        keep Wallace on his bed
                with nothing to do but think.
All round him, specimens waiting.
        Through gaps in the hut walls
                winged life in flight, hunting,
                        fighting, mating, laying eggs.

How is the planet, then, not overrun?
        Disease.
                Enemies.
                        Famine.
But: “Why do some die and some live?”

Beyond sight, that active volcano.

Tracts of ‘batu-angas’, burnt rocks,
        from peak to black-sand shore.

Such sudden terrors part
        of the huge slow changes.

# XXII

"...all living things were not made for man. Many of them have no relation to him. The cycle of their existence has gone on independently of his, and is disturbed or broken by every advance in man's intellectual development; and in their happiness and enjoyments, their loves and hates, their struggles for existence, their vigorous life and early death, would seem to be immediately related to their own well-being and perpetuation alone, limited only by the equal well-being and perpetuation of the numberless other organisms with which each is more or less intimately connected."

– Alfred Russel Wallace, *The Malay Archipelago*

*On seeing a bird of paradise at the*
*Walter Rothschild Zoological Museum, Tring*

Though shut in a glass case,
the "cinnebar red" of delicate
downy feathers stirs –
as if no place could keep out
enough of the open air,
ever, to deaden their grace.

Half a globe away, the lek
is "filled with waving plumes".
Male birds hang like flowers,
iridescent, whispy as mist,
then right themselves, and leap,
and call, drawing females in.

Every rise and fall of the sea,
every river, ravine, rock-face,
every thousand metres of mountain
offers a chance for change,
the wonder of new kinds.

Pulses of living matter
pressing forward always.

Of these, we too have come –
a way for the world to witness,
at last, its own transformations,
human civilisations never
so safe as to shut out the breath
of origins moving within us.

Wallace specimen: bird of paradise feathers

Natives of Aru shooting the great bird of paradise

## XXIII

"This is, I believe, the first instance of a 'flying frog', and it is very interesting to Darwinians as showing, that the variability of the toes which have been already modified for purposes of swimming and adhesive climbing, have been taken advantage of to enable an allied species to pass through the air..."

– Alfred Russel Wallace, *The Malay Archipelago*

There where bearded pigs
wallow, pooled rain
clears between-times, tepid
and still: tadpoles
root for scraps in the mud.

But their genes have begun to dream
of climbing, of gliding aslant
from towering upright to upright,
air resisting taut skin
between toes and fingers, body
suddenly light, big eyes
steering for safe landing.
Then climbing, climbing, metre
on vertical metre, canopy
swaying up there in the light.

Where its haunches will gather
ready to spring on winged
landings, on crawlings, but hidden
in its own tense stillness:
"deep shining green" among deep
shining green; from below,
yellow in that lofty brightness.

Light-box and magnifier
have me crouched, holding
my breath. This creature wasn't
believed in. I wish I could sense
in myself some transformation –
millions of years off, even –
something adequate to dimensions
not yet begun, or dreamt of.

Flying Frog

# XXIV

"...no organ, no sensation, no faculty arises before it is needed, or in a greater degree than it is needed."
– Alfred Russel Wallace, *The World of Life*

Coming in, after bottle-feeding
the weakling lamb,
my body retains
an echo of doing it –
my shoulder hunched to the bottle,
my breast supporting the head.

Now that I've looked again
at the Vestoniče Venus,
I see her afresh.
See how her shoulders hunch
to make those hollows
above the collar-bones,
how her hands are slipped underneath
long breasts heavy with milk,
ready to offer the nipples
to unseen mouths.

And yes, the man or woman
whose fingers modelled the clay
is present there too –
in these observations,
and in the soft bulge
of her hips, so wide and strong
over the tight sash
(the navel a little distorted),
the way clay is smoothed
to a shine of skin,
above all how the featureless head,
a closed bud,
waits to flower
as a human face –
this or that known one.

All other hominid kinds
        already extinct
                when she's laid to harden in fire.

I see how the tiny figure,
        four and a half inches high –
in a pouch at someone's belt,
        at the sacred tribal site,
                by a restlessly dreaming head –
might sow the seed of continuance.
        An impulse towards survival.
                Desires to hold in mind
                        through the flux and reflux of ice.

The Venus of Vestoniče

# NOTES & ACKNOWLEDGEMENTS

I am grateful to the naturalist Colin Titcombe, author and editor of publications exploring Gwent's wildlife, for being the first to draw my attention to Alfred Russel Wallace and for inviting me to write the forword to a collection of essays, *Wildlife in Gwent Post Millennium,* indicating the importance to all naturalists of Wallace's pioneering work. Wallace's own voice enters the sequence not only through quotations at the head of each poem but also through phrases in quotation marks within the poems themselves. During the writing of the sequence I was also encouraged and helped by other scientists willing to share their knowledge and show me some of their own or Wallace's specimens. My first such contact was with Dr. George Beccaloni, curator of orthopteroid insects in the Department of Entomology at The Natural History Museum, London. I could not have been more fortunate, since in George I found not only an enthusiast for Wallace but a scientist willing to show me specimens, advise me, and even read these poems as they developed. By George I was helped to discover new perspectives and avoid errors. In the library of the NHM I contemplated Wallace's detailed drawings of Amazonian fish, rescued by their author from a disastrous shipwreck, and by chance I was present when the NHM's Wallace Collection was displayed, shortly after its acquisition, to members of staff and a few lucky guests like myself. At the NHM, I met the Danish entomologist Dr. Torben B. Larsen, whose eloquent hand-mime of butterfly mating behaviour suggested a passage in one of the early poems. During a visit to the Bird Group at the Natural History Museum at Tring I was enabled to see Wallace's bird specimens, while a poem was also inspired by the mounted specimen of a bird of paradise nearby in the Victorian Natural History Museum set up by Lionel Walter Rothschild. On several occasions, I visited Kew and its Herbarium: I am grateful to Dr. Amelia Baracat, Latin America Research Fellow and Project Coordinator, Dr. Alec Pridgeon and Dr. David L. Roberts, Senior Scientific Officer, currently Hrdy Fellow in

Conservation Biology at Harvard, from all of whom I learned something of the strange habits of orchids and their pollinators. Dr. Alan Gregg of The Swansea Botanical Complex, Singleton Park, showed me *Epidendrum fragrans SW* in flower and helped me to improve my description of it. For their interest in this project, I have to thank Prof. and Mrs. David Collard, John and Jan Barrow, Andrew Geoffrey Mein and The Usk Civic Society, which also, with financial support from The Wallace Memorial Fund set up by Dr. Beccaloni, enabled the establishment, in 2006, of a memorial to Wallace near his birthplace beside the river Usk at Llanbadoc – a block of carboniferous limestone containing fossils and bearing a description of its age and significance donated by Dr. Tom Sharpe, Curator (Paleontology and Archives) in the Department of Geology of The National Musum of Wales, Cardiff. During the associated celebration in Usk of Wallace's life, Dr. Beccaloni spoke movingly about the great naturalist's life and work, while Wallace's grandson, Richard Wallace, gave the inaugural address at the unveiling of the stone, and has since encouraged me by his warm-hearted response to these poems in draft form. To Graham Harris I am grateful for his invitation to speak in 2005 about Wallace and the Batu-Angas project to The Usk Conservation and Environmental Group. I am indebted to Dr. Charles H. Smith of Western Kentucky University for his outline of Wallace's life and work, written especially for this book and encapsulating so much of what makes Wallace such an attractive thinker. Towards the end of this project I came into contact with the photographer Fred Langford Edwards, who invited me to collaborate with him in a series of exhibitions exploring the work of Wallace, bringing together his images (researched and made with support from a Wellcome Trust Award) and my poetry – a most interesting opportunity to extend my understanding of the great naturalist. The poets Hilary Llewellyn-Williams, Myra Schneider, Fiona Owen – who has taught Wallace for the Open University and is currently researching ecopoetics – and Dilys Wood have supported this project from its inception, and my husband, Walter Freeman Jackson, encouraged me throughout by his enthusiasm for Wallace and for the wonders of nature. Any remaining errors or infelicities are of course my own.

The project would have been significantly restricted without the support of a bursary from The Arts Council of Wales.

The first three of these poems won the Second Light Poetry Competition, 2000, judged by Mimi Khalvati. Others have appeared in *New Welsh Review*, *Planet*, *Quattrocento* and *Scintilla*, and in the anthologies *Into the Further Reaches* and *Making Worlds*.

Last but not least, my thanks to Amy Wack, my editor at Seren, for her unfailing encouragement and insight, and to Mick Felton for his determination that this book should echo, through its visual images, Wallace's love of nature.

# PICTURE ACKNOWLEDGEMENTS

National History Museum, London, by permission of the Trustees: p.16, 30, 45; p.28: A bee chafer beetle (*Trichius fasciatus*) on a bugle flower. Photographed at Kenfig Burrows, Wales, and p.48 A four spot orb weaver spider (*Araneus quadratus*) feeding on a dragonfly. Photographed at Wicken Fen, Cambridgshire, England. © George Beccaloni; p..36 and p.40: © Oxford Scientific; National Museums Loiverpool (World Museum): p.65; University Museum of Zoology, Cambridge: p.68. The photographs on pages 45, 65 and 68 were taken by Fred Edwards. The drawings on pages 39 and 42 are from *Travels on the Amazon* by Wallace (1892 edtion); on page 24 from *The Naturalist on the Aamazons*, H.W. Bates' account of the 1848 expedition (1884 edition); on pages 38, 61, 62, 69, 71 from *Malay Archipelago* by Wallace, 1906 edition.

# THE AUTHORS

Anne Cluysenaar was born in Belgium, daughter of the Belgian sculptor-painter John Cluysenaar. The family moved to Britain just before the outbreak of World War II. Educated at Trinity College, Dublin and Edinburgh University, she became an Irish citizen in 1961 and for many years taught literature, linguistics and creative writing. Widely published, she has written texts for opera, songs and son et lumieres, founded two literary journals and edited the selected poems of James Burns Singer and of Henry Vaughan. Her titles include *Timeslips: New and Selected Poems* (Carcanet, 1997). She currently edits poetry for *Scintilla* and has lived in Wales for the past twenty years, running a smallholding near Usk.

Charles Smith is a librarian, geographer and historian of science who works at Western Kentucky University in Bowling Green. He maintains the extensive 'Alfred Russel Wallace Page' on the Web: http://www.wku.edu/smithch/index1.htm